A Personal Tour of
LA PURISIMA

ROBERT YOUNG

L LERNER PUBLICATIONS COMPANY · MINNEAPOLIS

Cover: *An adobe stove is the centerpiece of La Purísima's kitchen, where neophyte cooks prepared meals for mission residents.*
Title page: *This painting from the late 1800s reflects the decayed state of La Purísima, which had passed through a number of owners before finally being abandoned.*

Many thanks to La Purísima docents Jenniveve Hutchinson, Fran Eggers, Billy Henry, Marie Schlueter, Fred Summerson, and Bob Wenk for sharing their passion for the past; to Karen Chernyaev and Chris Dall for their editorial assistance; and to Sara and Tyler Young for their willingness to explore new places. Special thanks to La Purísima rangers Joe McCummins and Steve Schuler-Jones, whose interest and expertise helped make this book come alive.

For Matthew and Miriam Lynch, supportive from the start.

Copyright © 1999 Robert Young

Website address: www.lernerbooks.com

LIBRARY OF CONGRESS CATALOGING-IN-PUBLICATION DATA

Young, Robert, 1951–
   A personal tour of La Purísima/ Robert Young
      p. cm. – (How it Was)
   Includes index.
   Summary: Presents a tour of this Spanish-built mission
in California from the point of view of a priest, two Chumash Indian
residents, and two military officers.
   ISBN 0-8225-3576-9 (lib. bdg. : alk. paper)
   1. Mission La Purísima Concepcíon (Calif.)—Juvenile literature.
   2. Chumash Indians—Missions—Juvenile literature.
   3. Missions—California—Juvenile literature. [1. Mission La Purísima
Concepcíon (Calif.) 2. Chumash Indians—Missions. 3. Indians of North
America—California—Missions. 4. Missions—California.] I. Title.
   II. Series.
   E99.C815Y68   1999
   979.4'91—DC21   97-46908

Manufactured in the United States of America
1 2 3 4 5 6 – JR – 04 03 02 01 98 99

Contents

Restored without any drawing of the original structure, the belltower at La Purísima is one of the mission's most identifiable features.

La Purísima was in style, dimensions and decoration the most modest of the Mission chapels in California. —Jessie S. Hildrop

Introduction

La Purísima was one of the 21 **missions** that missionaries (religious teachers) from Spain built between 1769 and 1823 on land that later became the state of California. La Purísima's full Spanish name is Mision la Purísima Concepcíon de Maria Santísima. This means "the Mission of the Immaculate Conception of Mary the Most Pure."

The purpose of the missions was to expand the Spanish empire in North America. Spain had already established a strong base in **New Spain** (modern-day Mexico) and was looking to create a permanent colony in California, which Spanish expeditions had explored in 1542 and 1602. The government of the colony of New Spain, based in Mexico City, worked with leaders of the Roman Catholic Church to create missions and presidios, or forts, along the Pacific coast, from Baja (lower) California to Alta (upper) California.

Priests of the Franciscan religious order baptize an Indian child. The Franciscans believed that baptism was the first step in converting native peoples to a Christian way of life.

The Spanish government believed that the mission system was the best way to get the Native Americans living in the area to become loyal Spanish citizens and Christians. **Franciscan** priests worked to convert the Indians to Christianity and to teach them to accept Spanish ways. The Franciscan priests were also in charge of running the mission. Soldiers at the missions were responsible for protecting the priests and for ensuring Indian obedience.

The missionaries used a ritual called baptism to welcome native peoples to their religious community. After being baptized, the Indians were referred to as neophytes, a Greek word meaning "newly converted." The Franciscans expected the neophytes to live at the mission and to learn a variety of skills—including farming, weaving, and ironwork—to maintain the daily operation of the mission. The Spanish plan was that over time the neophytes would learn to run the missions on their own.

La Purísima, the eleventh mission established by the Spaniards in Alta California, was one of four built along the central coast. Franciscans chose the site in 1787 after surveying the region. The inland location was a fertile area of low, rolling hills and grassy valleys dotted with oak trees and shrubs. In spring 1788, soldiers and workers began to build the mission. The site of the mission, at the base of some small hills just south of the Santa Inez River, is within the present-day city of Lompoc.

At that time, a Native American group known as the Chumash lived in the area. The Chumash were a self-sufficient society that was organized into communities of a few hundred people. The bountiful surroundings of the central coast provided them with plants, nuts, berries,

Before the arrival of the Spaniards, the Chumash Indians of California's central coast lived in grass-covered dwellings. Chumash villages typically numbered several hundred people.

small game, and fish. The Chumash expressed their thanks for this bounty by offering gifts to the earth and the sun, the two life forces that they considered sacred and deserving of honor.

The Chumash became members of the mission for several reasons. Some were curious. The missionaries lured others with gifts of red beads and cloth. When the Chumash lost much of their hunting and food-gathering areas to mission farms and ranches, many Indians joined the system so they would have enough to eat. Spanish soldiers took others from their villages and forced them to live at the mission. Still, many Chumash stayed away from La Purísima and continued to live in their villages.

La Purísima grew steadily. By 1804 nearly 1,500 people were living and working in the mission's **adobe** (clay) buildings. More than 20,000 head of livestock grazed on the mission's pastureland. Neophytes produced tanned cattle hides, wool, soap, and candles, and these goods enabled the Franciscans to establish trade networks with local Spanish settlers and visitors. Cattle hides and tallow—a waxlike substance made from animal fat—were especially popular with traders from New England, who offered manufactured goods in return.

Despite its growth, La Purísima did have problems. The Chumash were unaccustomed to the mission's strict daily routine, which was far different from their own. Forced to give up their traditional ways, many Chumash were not happy living at the mission. The soldiers punished those who tried to return to their villages. Many Chumash died from diseases, such as smallpox and measles, unknowingly brought to the mission by the Spaniards.

The earthquake that hit in 1812 completely destroyed the original mission and created a huge scar in the earth.

More trouble came in 1812, when a violent earthquake shook the area. The mission buildings were badly damaged. Heavy rains followed the earthquake, washing away adobe structures as well as any hope of repairing the mission.

La Purísima had to be totally rebuilt. But where should they build the new mission? The Franciscans chose a site about four miles to the northwest, across the Santa Inez River, in a place known as the "Valley of the Watercress." This site had many advantages, including a better water supply and a better climate. The new location was also closer to El Camino Réal, the main road that people used to travel to other missions.

La Purísima

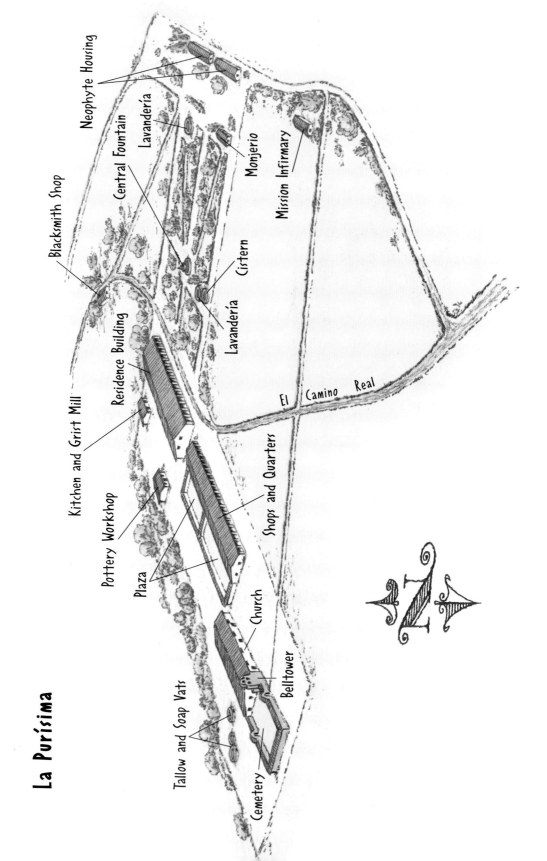

Neophyte Housing

Lavandería

Central Fountain

Monjerio

Mission Infirmary

Blacksmith Shop

Cistern

Lavandería

Kitchen and Grist Mill

Residence Building

El Camino Real

Pottery Workshop

Shops and Quarters

Plaza

Church

Tallow and Soap Vats

Belltower

Cemetery

People began living at the mission in 1813, but building went on until 1823. The new La Purísima had a different layout than other missions had. Most of the California missions were designed as a quadrangle, a four-sided shape with an open area in the middle. The buildings of the new La Purísima, however, were laid out in a long row. This design would make it easier for people to escape if another earthquake took place. The walls of the new mission were also made much thicker than those of the original mission, so that they could withstand another quake. Workers also built a blacksmith shop, a weaving room, storehouses, and new vats for holding soap and tallow.

The mission remained at this new site. There wasn't another major earthquake, but there were difficult times. The government of New Spain sent few supplies, and neophytes had to work hard to provide items for the mission and for trade. The mission suffered many setbacks, including fires and drought. Despite these problems, the mission eventually became entirely self-supporting.

Padre (father) Mariano Payéras was the head priest at La Purísima. He was also the father-president, or leader, of all the missions in California. Instead of moving to the mission in Carmel, where the mission government was usually located, Payéras stayed at La Purísima, which he preferred. He cared about the neophytes, and they liked him. But, like other mission leaders, Father Payéras believed he knew what was best for the Indians despite the suffering and hardships of mission life.

Come along as we take a closer look at La Purísima. It is a cool, crisp morning in April of 1820. The sky will soon lighten . . .

*The spare furnishings in the bedroom of Father Mariano Payéras
(inset) reflected his simple lifestyle.*

*He was personally a popular man on account of
his affable manners, kindness of heart, and
unselfish devotion to the welfare of all.*

—Hubert Howe Bancroft

With Father Payéras

Father-president Mariano Payéras slept soundly in his bedroom. Although the padre had a position of great power—he was the leader of all the California missions—his room was small and modestly furnished. He slept on a cot made from wood. In the corner of the room stood a washstand that held a bowl and a pitcher filled with spring water. Nearby were a plain wooden desk and chair.

As the first morning light appeared, Father Payéras opened his eyes and heard a rooster crow. Then another. The hour was early—about 5:00 A.M.—but it was time for him to get up. The padre had a great deal of work to do.

Father Payéras was one of two Franciscan priests at La Purísima. The other was Father Antonio Rodriguez. The two padres managed the mission. They were in charge not only of making the neophytes into good Christians and citizens of Spain but also of ensuring that they received

food, clothing, and shelter. Both priests taught the neophytes Spanish and made sure they went to church ser-
vices every day. They also saw to it that the neophytes
learned the trades necessary for the survival of the mission. Like all mission priests, the padres believed that
their role was to save the native peoples of Alta California
from what they felt was an unwholesome existence.

The morning air was chilly, so Father Payéras stirred
the coals in his small copper heating stove. Dressing
quickly, he pulled the traditional Franciscan gray habit
over his head. The hooded woolen cloak was rough and
scratchy, but it kept him warm. Payéras tied a rope belt
around his waist. As he strapped leather sandals onto his
feet, a knock came from the door.

It was Miguel, the padre's assistant. Like the other neo-
phytes, Miguel was a Chumash Indian who had received a
Christian name when the Franciscans had baptized him.
Miguel was holding a cup of thick, sweet hot chocolate
called *champurrado*. After exchanging greetings, Father
Payéras took the steaming cup from his young assistant.

*Father Payéras handled all
correspondence with other
California missions in his
office, which included a
desk and a bookcase.*

Sun shines through the thick adobe columns of the restored long porch, a corridor that runs along the residence building.

He carried the hot drink into the next room, his office, and walked over to his desk.

Father Payéras had a busy day ahead of him. There were many letters to read from the other missions in Alta California. As the father-president, he had to write reports on the state of the missions and send them to the government in Mexico City. The padre also had to teach class for the young neophytes at La Purísima. In addition, he was awaiting the arrival of a trader from New England, from whom he would try to obtain goods for the mission. Father Payéras hoped he might have time at the end of the day to work on a book that he was writing about Indian languages. At the moment, however, he had to prepare for Mass, the daily religious celebration.

He stepped out of his office and onto the long porch, a covered corridor that ran along the residence building housing the priests' quarters and other rooms. The roof of the long porch was held up by thick adobe columns. As he breathed in the morning air, the padre smelled the fresh scent of sage. This useful, fragrant plant grew wild around the mission. Bunches of cut sage hung along the roof of the corridor to dry. People at the mission used the dried sage as a medicine, a food spice, and as a way to make rooms smell good.

Ringing bells soon broke the quiet of the morning, waking those still asleep. Through the openings between the thick columns of the long porch, Father Payéras looked out at the colorful spring flowers blooming near the *lavanderías* (laundry areas). Spring was a special time of year. Although he was tired from his journeys to other

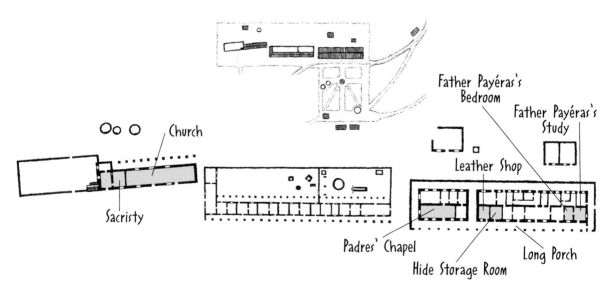

La Purísima was equipped with two lavanderías. These large troughs were used for bathing and washing clothes. Water from nearby springs was filtered and stored in a springhouse, a small structure built over the springs. From there the water flowed to the mission through pipes made from clay. Some of the water went to the central fountain, where it was used for drinking water. The rest flowed to the lavanderías.

The neophytes took baths every day in the lavandería farthest from the priests' quarters. The Spaniards used the closest one. But because the Spaniards believed taking baths would make them sick, they only took one or two baths a year.

The priests' private chapel, located in the residence building, duplicates the larger church where daily Mass was held.

missions, springtime raised his spirits. It was a time of renewal and growth.

Father Payéras walked along the porch of the residence building, passing barred windows and heavy wooden doors. These safeguards protected mission residents from the grizzly bears that lived in the area. He passed the dining area, the meeting room, and Father Rodriguez's quarters. As he continued along, he picked up the familiar scent of leather from the leather shop. This pleasant aroma gave way to the stink of rotting flesh that came from the next room, which stored cattle hides. When he reached the priests' private chapel, he stepped inside to say his morning prayers. After he was finished, he continued on his way to the church.

The padre next walked along the porch of another long structure, the shops and quarters building. This building housed the workshops where neophytes made candles, cloth, and furniture. The workshops were quiet now, but later in the morning the rooms would be buzzing with activity. This building also contained the quarters of the *mayordomo* (the mission foreman) and the quarters of the soldiers. The padre stepped off the porch at the end of the building and watched as a soldier raised the Spanish flag up the tall, narrow wooden pole. The bright red-and-yellow flag rippled in the early morning breeze.

The red-and-yellow flag flown at the mission was the Spanish flag that dated from the period.

The church was in sight. So was the belltower and the small cemetery where the mission residents buried their dead. Father Payéras paused as he admired these latest additions to the mission. Then he walked to the sacristy, a small room in the church where the padres prepared for Mass. He pulled open a drawer of the large wooden cabinet that held his vestments—the colorful cloaks he wore to perform Mass. The padre changed out of his habit and into his purple vestment. He began to arrange the items he would need for the service.

Soon Father Rodriguez entered the sacristy. Two young neophytes who would serve as acolytes, or helpers, for the Mass accompanied him. The padres talked to the boys and went over their duties with them.

The church sacristy housed the padres' vestments and the sacred vessels that they used to perform Mass for the neophytes.

The three bells at La Purísima were specially made for this mission. Workers in Lima, Peru, cast the bells in 1817 and 1818. Made of bronze, these bells were tuned so that the bellringer could produce many different sequences of tones. Each sequence had a different meaning—wake up, morning mass, mealtime, siesta (midday rest), or bedtime.

Ding-ding. Ding-ding. Ding-ding. The two-tone chiming of the mission bells called the neophytes to the church. It was six o'clock, time for morning Mass.

Musicians in a loft at one end of the church began playing a hymn on stringed instruments and wooden flutes. The choir picked up the melody. When the music began, the padres and the acolytes entered the church, where nearly 1,000 neophytes were chanting in a low hum.

Father Payéras looked out over the people. He was pleased so many Chumash had come to live at La Purísima, where he could teach them about God and about Spanish ways.

A statue of Mary, the mother of Jesus, sits above the altar in La Purísima's church.

*The Indians were to be Hispanicized not only in
religion but also in . . . virtually every other
aspect of their lives.* —James J. Rawls

With Rosa

Ten-year-old Rosa, a young neophyte, stood with
her mother, Maria, during Mass. The church was
crowded with other neophytes, and Rosa couldn't
see Father Payéras at the altar. Only when he
climbed the stairs to the pulpit could she get a
glimpse of the padre.

Rosa tried hard to listen to the padres as they
performed Mass. It wasn't easy because they only
spoke in her language—Chumash—some of the time. The
rest of the time they spoke Latin, a language that she
didn't understand very well.

The religion that the padres were teaching the neophytes was very different from the religion of Rosa's people. Her parents had told her about Chumash beliefs.
They believed in many gods instead of one. These gods
lived as spirits in plants, animals, and nature. Sometimes
the bad spirits lived in people, making them sick. Then

The pulpit was a raised platform from which the Franciscan priests gave the sermon during Mass. The pulpit at La Purísima was made of wood, but it looked like stone. The priests had workers paint the pulpit a greenish gray color to resemble the expensive marble pulpits in the great churches of Spain. The pulpit had a ceiling over it to help keep the speaker's voice from echoing. The ceiling, which looked like an umbrella, reminded the padres that a higher power was always above them.

the shaman—the Chumash holy man or holy woman—would have to drive the bad spirits away.

Rosa's parents had to be careful. Talking to her about the old beliefs angered the padres. They didn't want the neophytes to practice their old religion, and they punished those who did. Rosa thought this was unfair.

Although Rosa had a hard time understanding Mass, she liked being there. She loved the music, the singing, and the chanting. She especially liked being close to her mother. Rosa and the other unmarried neophyte girls didn't live with their families. They lived in the *monjerio,* a dormitory on the far side of the lavanderia where the *duana,* or teacher, taught girls how to become good wives. The duana also showed the girls how to weave wool into blankets, how to make leather into shoes, and how to know which plants were healthy to eat. Rosa knew it was important to learn such things. Yet, she wished she were living with her family.

Rosa stood up on her toes and stretched her neck, looking for her father and older brothers. They were standing on the other side of the church with all the other males. During Mass, the women and men were separated. The men always stood on the side of the church nearest the door. There was a reason for this—grizzly bears! The men stood by the doors to protect against bear attacks. Rosa remembered the last attack. The men had run outside and scared off the bear. Rosa had been frightened, but she was proud of her father and brothers.

When Mass ended, Rosa and her mother left the church and met the rest of the family outside, beneath the big oak tree. Together they walked to the plaza in front of the shops and quarters building. There they sat on the ground and ate *atole,* a gruel made from corn that the neophytes had grown. Atole was the morning meal eaten every single day. Rosa ate the warm porridge slowly, trying to make this

Unmarried neophyte women lived separately in the monjerio from the age of 10 until marriage. Neophyte families resided in two adobe buildings that were also located on the far side of the lavanderias. These buildings contained one-room apartments for each family. Other neophyte families lived in grass-covered houses spread over the mission grounds.

time with her family last. But the mayordomo, anxious to get the neophytes working, was pacing the area.

In a short time—too short for Rosa—the workday began. Every day except Sunday, the neophytes labored from early in the morning until sunset. Everyone had a job to do. Rosa's father, Carlo, made adobe bricks for building. Her mother, Maria, created candles in the candle shop. Rosa's brothers hoed weeds in the gardens and helped tan cattle hides into leather.

Rosa had two jobs to do. In the morning, she went to school with the other neophyte girls and learned math, church history, Latin, and Spanish from the padres. In the afternoon, her mother taught her how to make candles.

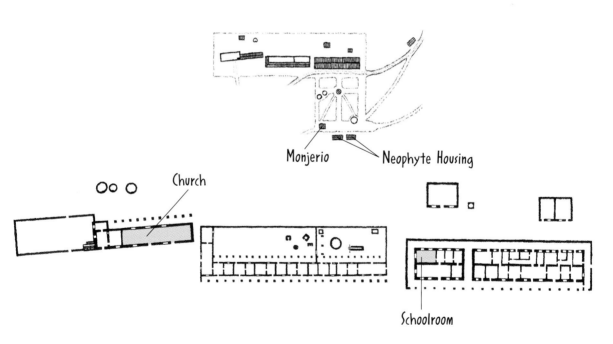

Monjerio   Neophyte Housing

Church

Schoolroom

Raising cattle was one of the most important industries at La Purísima. The meat from the cattle provided food, the fat was turned into tallow and used to make candles and soap, and the raw hides were traded and tanned into leather.

Male neophytes at La Purísima were responsible for making leather, a process that took several months to complete. First, they scraped the meat from the cattle hides. Then they cured the hides in a salty liquid to keep them from rotting. To dry the hides, they put them on wooden frames or used stakes to stretch them along the ground.

The next step was to soak the hides in water to remove the salt. After placing the hides in a solution of quicklime and water for three to four days, the neophytes scraped off the hair, washed the hides, and piled them into deep, brick-lined pits. Crushed oak bark was placed in between each hide, and the pits were filled with water.

The hides remained in the pits for three to six months. Afterward the neophytes washed them again and rubbed them with tallow or oil in the leather shop. After this final step, the hides became leather.

As Rosa made her way to the schoolroom in the residence building, she already missed her family. But she knew she would see them again at the noon meal, when they would eat *pozole* (a thick meat-and-vegetable soup) together. Later the family would gather with other neophytes in front of the mission buildings to visit and play games.

Rosa looked forward to watching her brothers play hoop and pole, a contest to see who could throw a pole or shoot an arrow through a rolling hoop. They were as good as the men at playing this game. Sometimes her brothers even won!

On her way to the schoolroom, Rosa climbed the steps to the residence building and walked the short distance to the doorway of the padres' chapel. She stopped and ran her hands along the smooth, wavy grooves in the thick wooden doors. Chumash artisans had carved these spaces to look like a flowing river.

The priests at La Purísima taught neophyte children how to read, write, and speak Spanish. The original intent of the mission priests had been to educate the native peoples in their own language. But the Chumash language had many different dialects and was tough to learn. In addition, the padres found it hard to teach the neophytes about Spanish life and Christianity in Chumash. The Chumash vocabulary did not contain words for ideas that the priests were trying to teach the neophytes.

Rosa's parents had told her the story of these doors. They were the "River of Life" doors, adorned with a design that her people had created long ago.

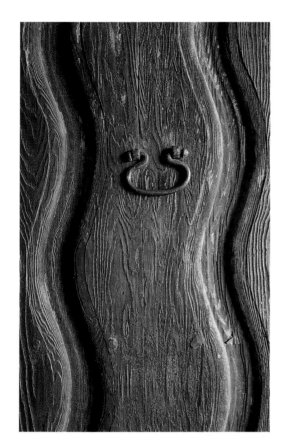

The river of life design, seen on other doors at La Purísima, was popular throughout the California missions. The padres believed that decoration was an aid to worship.

The design was a reminder that life is not always good and not always bad. No matter what happens, life goes on. Just like a river.

Rosa pushed open the heavy doors. As she walked through the padres' chapel, she could hear children talking and laughing. She quickly passed through the baptistry and into the schoolroom. Father Payéras smiled at Rosa as she found a place to sit among the other children on one of the long, wooden benches. It was eight o'clock—time to learn.

The mission barracks, located in the shops and quarters building, housed the sleeping and eating areas for mission soldiers.

It was agreed that Spanish regal authority and law must be the framework of Indian life.

—Edward Spicer

With Corporal Tapia

Corporal Tiburcio Tapia stood up as the late morning sun rose in the sky. The high ceiling and thick adobe walls helped cool his room and the others at La Purísima, even on warm days. This April day would be pleasant—about 70 degrees—not like the hot, dry time in late summer.

Corporal Tapia looked down at his red wool vest. The holes in it seemed to get bigger every month. He smoothed the vest then reached for his uniform jacket, which had faded from its original dark blue color. The red piping along the edges of the jacket was dull and frayed.

Tapia had hoped that he and the five soldiers under his command would be getting new uniforms. He had even spoken with Father Payéras about it this morning. But, once again, the padre told him there would be no new uniforms coming from Mexico City. There would be no new supplies or wages either.

The reason was simple, as Tapia knew. The colony of New Spain was fighting for its independence from Spain. The government of New Spain was spending most of its money on the war. As a result, the missions would suffer.

Corporal Tapia buttoned the shiny brass buttons on the front of his jacket. He adjusted his black head scarf, then straightened his shoulders, puffed out his chest, and lowered his chin. Despite the tattered uniform and the lack of supplies, Tapia was proud to be a soldier and a Californian.

Hat

Head Scarf

Cotton Shirt

Wool Vest

Jacket

Brass Buttons

Pantaloons

High Socks

A Soldier's Uniform

Leather Moccasins

Neophyte cooks used the estufa, *a three-hole stove made of adobe, to heat meals. Hot charcoal placed underneath the holes heated the clay pots on top of the stove.*

The soldiers under his command, though, were another story. Some of them had been picked off the streets of Mexico City. Others were criminals who had been sent to Alta California as punishment. These men were in a strange land far from home. They knew little about the Chumash and cared even less. The soldiers were tired of not being paid and of not being fed properly, and sometimes they took out their anger on the neophytes.

Tapia walked into the next room, the kitchen. It was warmer in there, and the smell of charcoal from breakfast was still in the air. The neophyte cook had used the charcoal to heat the soldiers' morning meal on the *estufa*, the three-hole stove made of adobe. The estufa now sat empty as the charcoal cooled.

When he reached the end of the kitchen, Tapia pushed open the door that led to the soldiers' quarters and went in. At the far end of the room was a jail cell, where a neophyte sat solemnly on the floor. His ankles were tightly fastened into heavy wooden stocks that prevented him from moving.

The neophyte was being punished for leaving the mission without permission. The soldiers had tracked him down. Leaving the mission without permission was against the rules. Even though some of the neophytes wanted to live freely in their old villages, the padres would not let them for fear that they'd return to Chumash ways.

Corporal Tapia was surprised and angry to see the man being held. He should have been taken out of the stocks hours ago. Tapia shouted out the window to Lopez, one of his soldiers, who was saddling a horse. Lopez quickly came into the soldiers' quarters, unlocked the stocks, and lifted them off the man's ankles. The neophyte was released from the stocks, but he was not free. To keep him from running away again, the soldiers would make him wear horse hobbles while he worked in the fields.

Lopez placed a piece of rounded metal around each of the man's ankles. Then he pushed a foot-and-a-half long rod through the holes in each of the rounded pieces. He locked the rod in place and pulled the Indian to his feet. The neophyte was able to walk, but the bar would keep him from running away.

As Lopez led the man outside to begin his workday, Corporal Tapia looked with satisfaction at the empty jail cell. Unlike many of the other soldiers, he liked the neophytes and did not enjoy punishing them. But he was responsible for keeping order at La Purísima and had to make sure the rules were followed.

Tapia inspected the soldiers' quarters as he slowly walked back toward the kitchen. The cots that lined the room were in order, with blankets neatly folded on them. The men's personal belongings were out of sight in their storage trunks. Shields, whips, and weapons hung in their proper places on the wall.

The thick wooden table near the door that led to the kitchen had been cleared shortly after breakfast, leaving

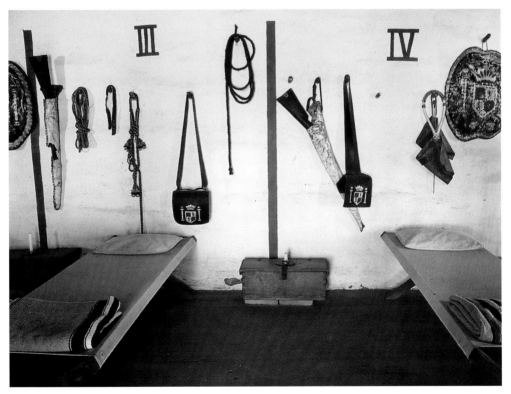

The sparse soldiers' quarters included wooden cots and pegs on which the men hung items such as whips, rifles, and shields.

only candles and a bowl of fruit. Tapia looked for the playing cards that were often sitting on the table. They had been moved to a shelf nearby. Knowing how much his men loved playing cards, Tapia had sensed that the cards would not be far away.

It was time for the corporal's ride. His chestnut-brown mare was saddled and waiting, but Tapia was not quite ready. He pulled on the leggings that would protect his legs, strapped on his sword, and grabbed his wide-rimmed hat. Outside the horse was swatting flies with his tail. Corporal Tapia climbed into the stirrups, patted the horse's coarse mane, and gently nudged him with his heels.

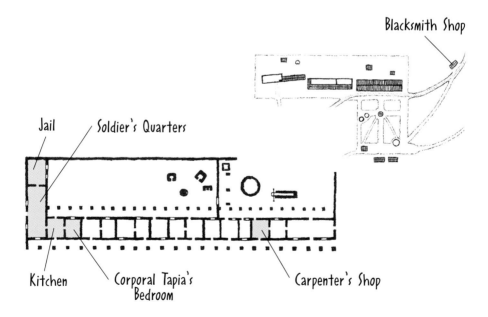

Blacksmith Shop

Jail Soldier's Quarters

Kitchen Corporal Tapia's Bedroom Carpenter's Shop

The carreta, *an ox-pulled cart, was a common means of transporting goods and people during mission times.*

The horse trotted northwest, in front of the shops and quarters building. Tapia passed some neophytes and an ox pulling a *carreta* (cart) full of wood that had been cut from the forest. The neophytes were taking the cart to the carpenter's shop, where workers would make the wood into tables, doors, and other useful items for the mission.

In front of the priests' quarters, neophytes carried dried hides to put into the storage room, where they would be kept until leather crafters cut, hammered, and sewed them into moccasins, sacks, harnesses, saddles, and even ropes.

Corporal Tapia stopped at the blacksmith shop and quickly dismounted from his horse. Clang, clang-clang.

Clang, clang-clang. Inside, blacksmiths hammered metal into all sorts of objects—nails, hinges, locks, keys, knives, hoes, and plows. Tapia could feel the heat from the forge (furnace) where blacksmiths warmed the metal until it was soft enough to mold.

The blacksmiths were very important at La Purísima. Not only did they make tools and weapons, they fixed them, too. Yesterday Corporal Tapia had left his musket to be repaired. It was ready to be picked up. Tapia took the gun outside, loaded it, and fired. It worked fine.

Tapia remounted his horse and rode northward, past neophytes hoeing weeds in the fields of wheat and corn. It wasn't long before he reached Nuñoz, another one of his men. Nuñoz was patrolling for a bandit who had been stealing cattle from the mission's herd. The bandit may have been a poor Spanish settler looking for something to trade or maybe a hungry Chumash from a nearby village. Whoever it was, Colonel Tapia and his men had to keep the thief from stealing again.

Nuñoz straightened in his saddle and pointed across the valley. He pointed to a man on horseback riding quickly into the dense underbrush. Nuñoz and Tapia pulled out their muskets, spurred their horses to a gallop, and raced after him.

When they got to the spot where they had seen the man, all they could find were hoof prints that led into the hills. Tapia and Nuñoz followed the prints for a long time, until they were sure the man was far from their cattle. Tapia looked at the sun and realized that it was past noon. It was time to get back to the mission. They would capture the bandit another day.

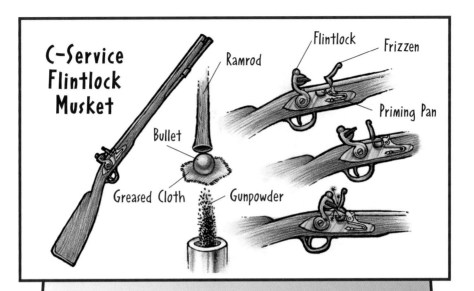

C-Service Flintlock Musket — Ramrod, Bullet, Greased Cloth, Gunpowder, Flintlock, Frizzen, Priming Pan

At three-and-a-half feet long, Corporal Tapia's C-service flintlock musket was shorter than most muskets, which were normally seven to eight feet long. The length made it easier to shoot while riding a horse.

Loading the musket was no simple matter. First gunpowder had to be poured down the barrel. Then a wad of greased cloth and a bullet were dropped into the barrel and pushed down using a ramrod.

In front of the flintlock was a metal piece called the frizzen. Under the frizzen was a small priming pan. The person loading the gun lifted the frizzen and put more gunpowder in the priming pan. When the flintlock was pulled back, the musket was ready to be fired. A skilled person could load a musket in about a minute.

When the trigger was pulled, the flintlock sprang forward, striking the frizzen and creating sparks. The sparks ignited the gun powder in the priming pan, which, through a small vent, lit the powder in the barrel. The resulting small explosion in the barrel forced out the bullet.

This adobe tallow vat is a replica of the original, which was built into the hillside behind the church.

The daily routine of the Indians' life was simple and uniform. —Helen Hunt Jackson

With Maria

The afternoon sun warmed Maria as she stood on the hillside, looking down on the church at La Purísima. She had eaten her midday meal with her family and then had taken a *siesta* (afternoon nap). Maria felt rested and ready to work.

Maria gazed down into the top of the large adobe vat, or tub, built into the hillside. The vat was filled with a whitish animal fat that Chumash workers had scraped from cow hides. A fire in the small pit under the vat heated the fat until it became tallow—a thick, soupy liquid. When the fire was put out, the tallow cooled and slowly hardened.

Maria moved forward to join the other workers who were ladling the soft, white substance from the vat. She knelt on the smooth stones that lined the rim of the vat and scooped the hot tallow into her large leather bag.

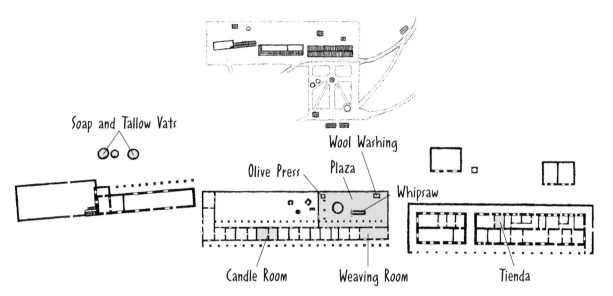

Soap and Tallow Vats

Olive Press

Wool Washing

Plaza

Whipsaw

Candle Room

Weaving Room

Tienda

With the tallow she collected, Maria would make candles. Other workers would use the tallow to make soap. The rest would be stored for later use or traded.

Maria carried the heavy bag on her back, walking behind the church and then along the shops and quarters building. She knew a shorter way to get to the candle room, but if she took that route she would have to pass the soldiers' quarters. Like many of the neophytes, Maria feared the soldiers and kept away from them as much as she could. Their large horses, sharp swords, whips, and loud guns made her shiver with fear. Many of the soldiers were cruel, too. They put her people into stocks or in jail. Sometimes the soldiers whipped them.

Maria carried her leather bag into the plaza, one of her favorite places at La Purísima. She liked watching all the activity that took place here. In one corner, women washed

In addition to candles, tallow was also used to make soap. Neophytes put tallow into a soap vat along with water and wood ashes. Then they heated the ingredients for several days. When the liquid cooled, soap floated on top of the water. Workers skimmed off the soap and poured it into a mold. When the soap hardened, it was taken out of the mold and cut into bars.

wool in large tubs while others dyed it in smaller pots. Across the way, workers pressed oil out of olives. In the center of the plaza, two men cut lumber with a whipsaw—a long, narrow saw with handles on both ends.

Maria then continued through the plaza and into the weaving room. Click-clack, click-clack, click-clack. The looms made a steady sound as the women moved them back and forth, weaving colorful cloth and blankets. Some women in the weaving room prepared the wool. Others spun it into yarn. Maria hoped there would be enough clothes and blankets for her people when winter came.

With spinning wheels and other devices, neophyte workers spun colorful cloth and blankets out of wool from sheep raised on mission grounds.

After she passed through the rounded doorway of the weaving room, Maria stopped in the corridor and set down her heavy bag. She would get her daughter Rosa from school and return for the bag on their way to the candle room.

In the schoolroom, Maria greeted Rosa with a smile. Maria pulled her daughter to her, smoothing Rosa's shiny black hair. She was glad her daughter could work with her. But Maria knew that they had a few stops to make before going to the candle room.

Rosa raced around the back of the residence building and past the pottery shop. Maria followed, trying to keep up with her daughter. At the adobe pit, Maria's husband, Carlo, and other Chumash men stomped water, straw, and clay into mud. Sweat dripped off the men as they poured the mud into wooden molds to dry into hard bricks. Maria could see that Carlo was tired. Making adobe bricks was hard work. Every day the men labored from dawn to dusk making several hundred bricks. The bricks would be used for building at La Purísima.

Maria and her daughter enjoyed watching the men, but they had work to do, too. Maria took hold of Rosa's hand, but the child had her own stop to make. She pulled Maria into the *tienda,* the trade store, where settlers in the area—as well as people living at the mission—could trade for all sorts of things.

Even though there were few supplies, Rosa loved looking around the trade store. She gazed at the brightly colored cloth and felt the smoothness of the hoes. Rosa always spent a little more time standing over the pieces of wrapped chocolate, sniffing to get just the slightest whiff of her favorite treat. Maria wished she had something to trade to get her daughter some chocolate, but she did not. She hoped Carlo could work tending cattle at a nearby ranch again. Then maybe he would be able to buy Rosa some treats.

Maria and Rosa left the tienda and slowly walked to the shops and quarters building. Maria picked up her bag of tallow and carried it along the corridor to the candle room, where two Chumash women were hard at work making candles. One was pouring hot tallow into a metal mold. The other woman was dipping wicks into a deep metal vat with tallow in it.

The priests at La Purísima sometimes contracted neophytes to work on the *ranchos* (ranches) of Spanish settlers in the area. Although the neophytes were not paid money for their work, they were given credit at the *tienda*.

Maria carried her bag over to a metal container placed over a smoldering fire. There was water at the bottom of the vat and several inches of liquid tallow on top of the water. While Maria emptied the hardened tallow from her bag into the vat, Rosa added wood to the fire. As they waited for the water to melt the newly added tallow, Maria showed Rosa how to tie strings to the arms of the wooden frame. The strings would be the candle wicks.

By the time Maria and Rosa had tied the wicks to the arms of the frame, the new tallow had melted and risen to join the thick layer on top of the water. It was time to make candles.

Maria grabbed the closest arm of the dipping frame and pulled it until it was over the vat of soft tallow. She

Neophytes at La Purísima used large leather bags (right) *to carry tallow to the candle room. The candle-dipping frame* (above) *allowed laborers to make many candles at one time.*

lowered the arm until the wicks were submerged in the vat. After a few seconds, she lifted the wicks out of the tallow by pulling up the arm of the frame. When she lifted the arm up, each wick was thinly coated with tallow. Maria rotated the frame and lowered the next arm.

After Maria had lowered each arm, she waited a few minutes as the tallow cooled and hardened on the wicks. Then it was Rosa's turn. Every time Rosa dipped the wicks into the vat, the coating of tallow got thicker and thicker.

After about an hour of dipping, the candles were finished. Maria showed Rosa how to untie the strings from the dipping frames. Next, they tied the candles to a rack on the other side of the room, where they would harden. In a few days, the tallow candles would be ready to use.

Maria's job took much skill. She had to dip the wicks for just the right length of time. She also had to maintain the temperature of the tallow in the tank. If the tallow was too hot, it would melt off the wicks. If the temperature was too cool, the tallow would be too hard to dip into. The candlemakers controlled the temperature with the amount of wood they put on the fire.

Maria looked over at the candles drying on the rack. Although making candles was a hot and greasy job, she was proud of her work, and it was better than most of the other jobs at the mission.

The windows at La Purísima were small and let in very little light. Many candles were needed to light the church as well as the other rooms at the mission. Each family received one candle a day to burn in their living quarters.

There were only a few candle-makers at La Purísima. They produced between 200 and 300 candles a day. Some of the candles used at La Purísima were made of beeswax, but most were made of tallow because animal fat was easier to obtain. Tallow candles were sticky to touch. They spat, burned very quickly (one-half hour to an hour), and left a pool of grease.

The large cross on the hillside told visitors that they were near the mission.

In the course of time, vessels began to come into the ports to trade with the missions . . . thus began the great trade of California.

—Richard Henry Dana Jr.

With Captain Roger

Captain John Roger was tired. He'd docked his trading ship, the *Eagle,* early this morning and immediately set out for La Purísima. It was late afternoon, and he'd been on a horse all day—first riding along the rugged trail that overlooked the ocean, then turning inland and traveling over many hills and passing several Indian villages. Captain Roger was ready to stop, but he hadn't ridden the final 15 miles to La Purísima yet.

Gonzalez, the Spanish soldier sent to escort Captain Roger from the mission, told him that it wouldn't be long. They would soon be at the mission. It couldn't be soon enough for the captain. After many months at sea, he liked being on land but not bouncing along a trail on the back of a horse.

The captain shifted his weight in the saddle and thought about the *Eagle.* The vessel was anchored in a small

Trade between the missions and visitors was technically illegal. The Spanish government, which feared the presence of foreign powers in Alta California, had forbidden the missions from trading with anyone but Spain. But Spanish supply ships were infrequent, and the missions often found it necessary to exchange goods with traders from the United States and other countries.

outpost port called Little Cojo Bay. His crew was busy cleaning the ship and making repairs. They were also pulling trade items out of storage, dusting them off, and chasing the rats away. They would take these goods ashore when he returned.

Captain Roger wondered what was worse—being away from his home and family in Boston, Massachusetts, for more than a year; sailing the dangerous southern route around Cape Horn, at the tip of South America; facing storms at sea; or riding on a horse for a day. He wasn't sure.

The captain suddenly spotted a wooden cross on a hillside. It was a landmark for the mission. He knew they must be close. But a moment later, he wasn't so sure. He saw a pinkish tower rising above the land. It looked like a belltower. This couldn't be La Purísima. He didn't recall the mission having a belltower. Could they be lost?

Gonzalez laughed. No, he told Captain Roger, they weren't lost. The *campanario* (belltower), as well as a cemetery, had been added since the captain's last visit.

The familiar long, low white buildings of La Purísima soon came into view. This is what he remembered from his last trading visit. The two men eased their horses into trots and rode toward the mission. There were many people in front of the buildings. Roger wondered what was going on.

The cemetery was the first part of the mission the two men reached. Captain Roger was happy to jump down from his horse after the long ride. He looked up at the belltower and then scanned the cemetery. He noticed quite a few headstones.

Before the Chumash came to La Purísima, they lived an average of 35 to 45 years. At the mission, their average lifespan dropped to 30 to 35 years. There were several reasons for this shorter life. The neophytes worked long and hard, with little hope of returning to their villages and living like their ancestors had. The Spaniards also brought many diseases, such as measles, chicken pox, and smallpox, and the mission infirmary had few medical supplies. The poor sanitation at the mission, the inferior diet, and the lack of clothes and blankets during the winter also affected the health of the neophytes. The cemetery *(above)* was adjacent to the church.

Captain Roger and Gonzalez walked their horses past the church. The area in front of the shops and quarters building was filled with neophytes. They had finished with their work for the day. It was early evening, a time to visit with family and to play games.

In the shade of the corridor, little girls played with dolls made of rags and cornhusks. Men, women, and children sat in small groups and played dice games. Men and boys ran up and down the field hitting a wooden ball with curved sticks. Others competed at hoop and pole. Captain Roger remembered this game from his previous visits to the mission.

Some children followed the captain at a distance. They seemed curious but shy. Their faces looked sad. Captain Roger stopped, reached into his saddlebags, and pulled out a small pouch. The children pushed close to him. In the pouch were tiny red beads made of glass. The captain had traded these beads with other native peoples. The captain passed the beads to the children, watching their eyes widen with interest.

The neophytes loved games. Some of the games they played were introduced by the Spaniards. Others were of Chumash origin. Gambling contests were especially popular. The neophytes loved making bets on a memory game called *wauri*. They also gambled on dice, which they made out of sticks and even walnuts. What did they bet? All sorts of things, including clothing, skins, beads, tools, and chores.

After all the beads had been handed out, Captain Roger and Gonzalez continued on to the padres' quarters. As they passed the herb garden, Roger wondered if the

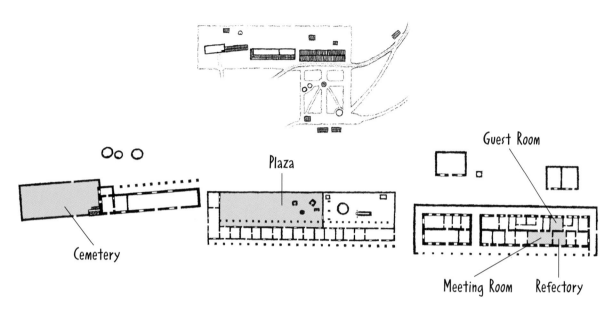

Guest Room

Plaza

Cemetery

Meeting Room   Refectory

padres had any dried rosemary or tansy to trade. The captain liked to throw these fragrant herbs on the floor of his cabin on the *Eagle*. They kept insects away and helped make the cabin smell good.

At the residence building they tied up their horses, and Gonzalez led the captain through the meeting room and into the guest room. The captain bent his head forward as he stepped through the low doorway.

The captain liked the guest room. It was huge, much larger than his cramped cabin on the ship. The room had two small windows, one with glass, the other covered with buckskin. While Gonzalez retrieved the captain's saddlebags, Roger stepped over to the small stand with the water pitcher and basin on it. He poured some water into the basin and splashed it on his face. It felt good to wash off the trail dust.

When Gonzalez returned, Captain Roger thanked his escort for the kind service. He pulled some tobacco from his saddlebag and handed it to the soldier. Gonzalez was pleased with the gift because tobacco was rarely grown at the mission.

After Gonzalez left, Captain Roger sat down on the four-poster bed in the corner. How strange it was going to be to sleep on a bed that wasn't moving to the rhythm of the sea! But there was no time to think about sleep. He'd come to the mission for a reason—to trade.

Tallow and hides were what the captain wanted the most. They would both bring good prices in Boston. He could also sell the colorful blankets that were made at the mission. Roger wondered if the padres had any food to trade. The Indians at the mission didn't look well fed, so the captain doubted whether there was extra food. Still his crew could use some dried beans and meat for their voyage home.

A knock at the door interrupted the captain's thoughts. A Chumash woman told him that dinner was ready. Roger followed her into the refectory, the dining room where the padres ate.

Father Payéras and Father Rodriguez greeted the captain warmly. As the Chumash woman served them pozole, the men talked about trading. Father Rodriguez mentioned that they had a lot of tallow, hides, and blankets. Roger told them what he had aboard his ship—metal that the blacksmiths could make into tools, as well as silk, spices, and sandalwood from China. He also had some statues and mirrors.

The padres were interested in the items the captain had to offer. Although no exchange would take place for a few days, they all agreed that a deal could be made. Roger would have to send word to his crew to bring the items to the mission.

After dinner, Roger returned to his room. He laid down on his bed as the daylight coming through his window faded around him. In a short time, he heard the bells calling the neophytes to evening Mass. Tomorrow he would attend morning Mass. That would please the padres.

Although the captain was very tired from his long day, he was glad he'd made the trip to La Purísima. He would try to make some good trades in the next few days. Then he would sail back home to Boston. Captain Roger looked forward to returning to his home.

Although the mission suffered through difficult times, the hard work of the neophytes and the establishment of a steady trade network enabled La Purísima to survive for nearly 10 years.

By the late 1800s, the mission had passed through many hands and was beginning to show signs of deterioration.

The most desolate ruin of all is that of La Purísima Mission. Nothing is left but one long, low adobe building, with a few arches of the corridor; the door stands wide open, the roof is falling in. . . . —Helen Hunt Jackson

Afterword

Life at La Purísima soon changed. All the missions had to pledge their loyalty to Mexico, which won its independence from Spain in 1821. The government sent even fewer supplies, so the neophytes had to work harder to provide food for the people living at the mission. Father Payéras, who was popular with the neophytes, died in 1823. The soldiers at the mission, who were still unpaid, grew more restless and angry. Some took out their anger by beating and abusing the neophytes.

In 1824 the neophytes revolted. A huge comet appeared in the sky, signaling to the Chumash a time of change and new beginnings. Joined by Chumash from other missions, the neophytes took control of La Purísima by force and held the mission for nearly a month.

To put down the revolt, the Mexican government sent more than 100 soldiers from the presidio at Monterey.

They fought the Indians and defeated them. One soldier died in the fighting, and two were wounded. Sixteen Chumash were killed, and many more were wounded. The Mexican government sentenced 7 Indians to death for leading the rebellion and imprisoned 18 others.

Meanwhile, settlers in Alta California had been complaining to the government that the missions held too much power and owned the best land. So in 1834 the Mexican government took the missions away from the Catholic church—a process known as **secularization.** The government hired mayordomos from Mexico to take charge and distribute the land among the neophytes and the settlers. But the mayordomos sent to La Purísima and other missions were corrupt. They stole mission property and gave much of the land to their families and friends.

Soon the neophytes were free to leave La Purísima, and many did. By 1844 only 200 neophytes remained at the mission. Some found work in towns or on nearby ranches but earned little pay. Because they had grown accustomed

In this nineteenth-century drawing, a mayordomo from Mexico urges neophytes to work. These officials, sent to run the mission after the Franciscans left, were often greedy and corrupt.

During the 1930s, workers from the Civilian Conservation Corps helped restore La Purísima, rebuilding many of the mission structures from scratch.

to mission life, the neophytes could not go back to their old ways. Many of the remaining neophytes were killed by a smallpox epidemic.

The loss of unpaid labor made it hard to keep the mission productive, and many of the buildings at La Purísima fell into disrepair. Only the residence building remained in good condition. During the 1800s, the building was used as a shelter for sheep and cattle, a blacksmith's shop, and even a saloon. By 1900 all of the buildings at La Purísima had fallen into ruin.

In 1903 the Union Oil Company, knowing there was a lot of oil in the area, bought the land where the mission once stood. Officials of the company eventually realized what an important landmark the mission was. They tried to get someone to restore La Purísima, but without success. The project would be too expensive.

It wasn't until 1934 that restoration of the mission began. The state of California had purchased the land and had engaged the Civilian Conservation Corps (CCC) and the National Park Service to rebuild the mission. When work began, only a few wall fragments and some pillars remained from the original structures. Workers photographed the ruins and used the pictures to help them recreate the mission buildings. It took a workforce that varied between 25 and 200 people seven years to complete the project. Workers made adobe bricks and clay roof tiles by hand, as the neophytes had done. The rebuilding effort—in terms of rebuilding from scratch—was one of the largest historical restoration projects in U.S. history.

Opened to the public in 1941, La Purísima is the most completely restored of all the California missions. All the mission's structures have been rebuilt to reflect the mission at its peak, and the grounds have been replanted to reflect the period. La Purísima's living history program, in which volunteers dress up and act the parts of people at the mission in 1820, draws more than 150,00 people each year.

Actors in La Purísima's living history program portray life as it was during the mission's heyday.

Glossary

adobe: A type of clay soil found in Mexico and in dry parts of the United States. In Alta California, workers formed wet adobe into bricks that hardened in the sun.

Franciscan: A member of the Order of Friars Minor, a Roman Catholic community founded in Italy by Saint Francis of Assisi in 1209. The Franciscans are dedicated to performing missionary work and acts of charity.

mission: A center where missionaries (religious teachers) work to spread their beliefs to other people and to teach a new way of life.

New Spain: A large area once belonging to Spain that included what would become the southwestern United States and Mexico.

secularization: A series of laws enacted by the Mexican government in the 1830s. The rulings removed control of the missions from the church and placed them in the control of the civil government.

Pronunciation Guide

adobe	ah-DOH-bee
Chumash	CHOO-mash
La Purísima Concepcíon de Maria Santísima	lah poo-REE-see-mah con-thep-thee-OHN day mah-REE-ah sahn-TEE-see-mah
lavandería	lah-vahn-day-REE-ah
monjerio	mohn-HAY-ree-oh
Payéras, Mariano	pay-EHR-ahs, mah-ree-AH-no

Further Reading

Behrens, June. *Missions of the Central Coast.* Minneapolis: Lerner Publications Company, 1996.

Gibson, Robert O. *The Chumash.* New York: Chelsea House Publishers, 1991.

Lee, Georgia. *A Day With a Chumash.* Minneapolis: Runestone Press, 1999.

Nelson, Libby and Kari A. Cornell. *Projects and Layouts.* Minneapolis: Lerner Publications Company, 1998.

Pelta, Kathy. *California.* Minneapolis: Lerner Publications Company, 1994.

Yamano, Linda. *Weaving a California Tradition.* Minneapolis: Lerner Publications Company, 1997.

Touring Information

La Purísima Mission State Historic Park is open from 9:00 A.M. to 5:00 P.M. everyday of the year except Thanksgiving, Christmas, and New Year's Day. The park is located four miles northeast of Lompoc, California, on Purísima Road. For more information about visiting the mission,

write to:
La Purísima Mission State Historic Park
2295 Purísima Road
Lompoc, CA 93436

or call:
(805) 733-3713

Index

About the Author

Robert Young, a prolific author of children's books, created the *How It Was* series to enable readers to tour famous landmarks through the experiences of people who did or may have lived, worked, or visited there. Robert, who makes his home in Eugene, Oregon, teaches elementary school and visits schools around the country to talk with students about writing and curiosity. Among his other literary credits are *Money* and *Game Day,* titles published by Carolrhoda Books, Inc.

Acknowledgments

For quoted material: p. 5, Paul Elder, *The Old Spanish Missions of California* (San Francisco: Paul Elder and Company Publishers, 1913); p. 13, June Behrens, *Missions of the Central Coast* (Minneapolis: Lerner Publications Company, 1997); p. 23, James J. Rawls, *Indians of California* (Norman, Oklahoma: University of Oklahoma Press, 1984); p. 31, Robert Heizer, "The Impact of Colonization on the Native California Societies," *The Journal of San Diego History,* Vol. 24, Winter 1978; p. 41, Helen Hunt Jackson, *Glimpses of California and the Missions* (Boston: Little, Brown, & Company, 1902); p. 49, Richard Henry Dana Jr., *Two Years Before the Mast* (New York: Harper & Brothers, 1840); p. 58, Helen Hunt Jackson, *Glimpses of California and the Missions* (Boston: Little, Brown, & Company, 1902)
For photos and artwork: Seaver Center for Western History Research, Natural History Museum of Los Angeles County, pp. 1, 9, 56; © Chuck Place, pp. 4, 12, 15, 19, 20, 22, 27, 35, 43, 46, 51, 55, 60; Independent Picture Service, pp. 6, 58; © Southwest Museum, p. 7; © Noella Ballenger, pp. 14, 33, 46 (inset), 47; © Jim Lundgren, pp. 17, 18, 21, 29; © Diane C. Lyell, pp. 24, 30, 37, 48; © Sherry Shahan, p. 40; La Purísima Mission State Historic Park, p. 59. All maps and artwork by Bryan Liedahl. Cover: © Chuck Place.